The Gifts Of The Spirit

Written and designed by Jane Goodwin

Illustrations by Eric Toner

Published in Canada by Worship With Us Ministries
International Standard Book Number: 978-1-7752467-4-9
www.worshipwithus.ca/books

Scripture quotations: Taken from the HOLY BIBLE: EASY-TO-READ VERSION
© 2001 by World Bible Translation Center, Inc. and used by permission.

THE GIFTS OF THE SPIRIT

When we ask Jesus to come into our hearts and to fill us with His Holy Spirit, He has gifts that He gives us. They are gifts we use in His power to show people how great and wonderful our God is.
We have all the gifts to use them as they are needed.

There are different kinds of spiritual gifts, but they are all from the same Spirit. There are different ways to serve, but we serve the same Lord. And there are different ways that God works in people, but it is the same God who works in all of us to do everything.
Something from the Spirit can be seen in each person. The Spirit gives this to each one to help others.
1 Corinthians chapter 12, verses 4 to 7

Gifts from Heaven?
What are they?

There are 9 gifts given to us by the Holy Spirit which can only be used in His power.

The "Gift of the Word of Wisdom."
The "Gift of a Word of Knowledge."
The "Gift of Faith."
The "Gift of Healing"
The "Gift of Miracles."
The "Gift of Prophecy."
The "Gift of Distinguishing of Spirits."
The "Gift of Tongues."
The "Gift of Interpretation of tongues."

The Spirit gives one person the ability to speak with wisdom. And the same Spirit gives another person the ability to speak with knowledge. The same Spirit gives faith to one person and to another he gives gifts of healing. The Spirit gives to one person the power to do miracles, to another the ability to prophesy, and to another the ability to judge what is from the Spirit and what is not. The Spirit gives one person the ability to speak in different kinds of languages, and to another the ability to interpret those languages. One Spirit, the same Spirit, does all these things. The Spirit decides what to give each one.

1 Corinthians chapter 12, verses 8 to 11

So many gifts! Let's open them!
Yeah!
INTERPRETATION
FAITH
WISDOM
TONGUES
MIRACLES
HEALING
PROPHECY
KNOWLEDGE
DISCERNMENT
LOVE

Word of Wisdom

In some situations we may need wisdom that we wouldn't ordinarily have. The Holy Spirit will give us wisdom when we ask Him and speak to us about what we need to do or say. It is His wisdom that comes from heaven to help us and others.... here on earth.

"Thank you God for giving us your wisdom from heaven, so that we know your will."

Which way shall we go?
What shall we do?
Let's ask God for His wisdom and He will tell us the way.

Word of Knowledge

A word of knowledge is knowing something we wouldn't know ourselves about a person or a situation. It is the Holy Spirit showing us what is happening with a person or a situation so we can pray and help one another.

"Thank you, God, for your word of knowledge to help those around us."

God told me
your dog is lost and it makes you sad.
Let's pray....

Faith

The gift of faith is when God gives us absolute certainty that a prayer will be answered and will come to pass. Even when others have a hard time believing a prayer will be answered, we know deep down that God will certainly come through.

"Thank you, God, for the gift of faith to believe you and trust you."

With the gift of faith from God, I KNOW there will be a church here one day.

Healing

The gift of healing is given to us to pray for a sick person and when we pray that person will be healed and well.

"Thank you, God, for your gift of healing."

Oh, I'm so sick!
Please pray for me
Thank You, Jesus!!

Miracles

The gift of miracles is for when it is impossible for something to happen in the natural. For example if someones leg is broken, it can heal naturally. However, if the leg is missing from the knee down, it would take a miracle for the leg to grow back. We can pray for miracles to happen when there is no natural way for something to happen.

"Thank you, God, for your wonderful miracles!"

In the name of Jesus, stand up and walk!
It's a miracle! Thank you, Jesus!

Prophecy

Prophecy is a message directly from God, given from one person to another for encouragement, strength, hope and comfort. When we speak a prophetic word to the church or to people it is to lift up, build up or cheer up.

"Thank you, God, for your prophetic words, that encourage, strengthen and make us happy."

This is what I
feel God is saying right now....

Discerning of Spirits.

The gift of discerning of spirits is so that we know whether we are sensing God, a person or something else. The Holy Spirit can show us what kind of spirit is at work.

"Thank you, God, for discernment to recognize what is your Holy Spirit and what is not."

God, show me which is speaking from Your heart and Your Spirit, and which is not....

Tongues

The gift of tongues is when the Spirit of God gives us the ability to pray in a language we haven't learned and we don't know or understand. It is a language from heaven between us and God. It strengthens us on the inside.

"Thank you, God, for a prayer language from your Spirit, to pray your will and to praise your name."

De a lo sema Jesus.
Remay sa to da moe

Interpretation of Tongues

When a prophetic message is given in tongues in a public place another person can give an understanding of that word. This is called an interpretation. This is so everyone will know what God has said. The person speaking in an unknown tongue can also bring the interpretation if God chooses to do it that way.

"Thank you, God, for giving me the gift of interpretation of tongues to make your words clear to everyone.."

Sai mea tura ba cora sha basa ca nai atoo
Let the children free. Loose them into my Spirit

Love

Scripture specifically tells us that if we have and use these nine gifts of the spirit but we use them without love, we are using them incorrectly.

"I may speak in different languages, whether human or even of angels. But if I don't have love, I am only a noisy bell or a ringing cymbal."
1 Corinthians chapter 13 verse 1

True love of God and people is what our walk with God is all about. Without love, using these gifts of the spirit are not important and mean nothing to God. Jesus loved us so much, he gave his life on the cross for us. It was and is unconditional love. If we don't walk in His love for the Father and for others these things have no value.

Jesus said,

"I give you a new command: Love each other. You must love each other just as I loved you. All people will know that you are my followers if you love each other."
John chapter 13, verses 34 and 35

So you see, God has equipped His children by His Spirit to see, speak and do the things that Jesus did. Loving God and loving people make using these spiritual gifts easy. We just need to ask the Father for the Baptism of the Holy Spirit and He is faithful to fill us, teach us, and use us for the glory of His kingdom.

you

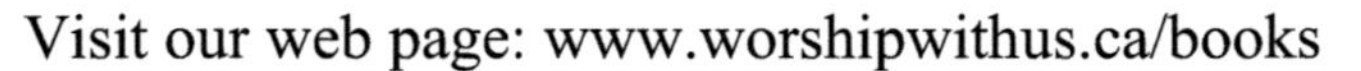

Visit our web page: www.worshipwithus.ca/books